SECOND EDITION

American Start with English

Student Book 1

D. H. Howe

OXFORD UNIVERSITY PRESS

Oxford University Press

198 Madison Avenue
New York, NY 10016 USA

Great Clarendon Street
Oxford OX2 6DP England

Oxford New York
Athens Auckland Bangkok Bogotá Buenos Aires
Calcutta Cape Town Chennai Dar es Salaam Delhi
Florence Hong Kong Istanbul Karachi Kuala Lumpur
Madrid Melbourne Mexico City Mumbai Nairobi Paris
São Paulo Singapore Taipei Tokyo Toronto Warsaw

and associated companies in
Berlin Ibadan

OXFORD is a trademark of Oxford University Press.

ISBN 0-19-434013-9

EDITORIAL MANAGER:	Shelagh Speers
EDITOR:	Edward Yoshioka
ASSISTANT EDITOR:	Lynne Robertson
PRODUCTION AND DESIGN:	OUP International Education Unit and Oxprint Design
ASSOCIATE PRODUCTION EDITOR:	Joseph McGasko
PRODUCTION MANAGER:	Abram Hall
COVER DESIGN:	April Okano
COVER PHOTOGRAPH:	Alan Kaplan
ILLUSTRATIONS:	Val Biro

Printing (last digit): 10 9 8

Printed in Hong Kong

Contents

Contents

American
Start with English

SECOND
EDITION

a book

a ball

1

a bag

a cat

an apple

an orange

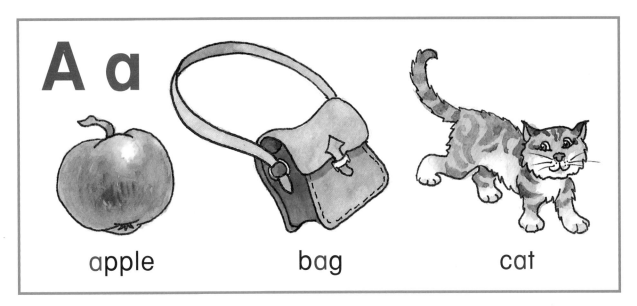

A a

apple   bag   cat

3

a box

a cup

4

a desk

B b

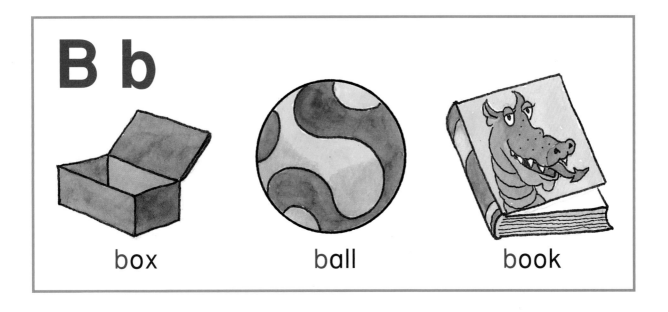

box   ball   book

It is a car.

It is a dog.

It is an umbrella.

C c		
cup	car	cat

It is a doll.

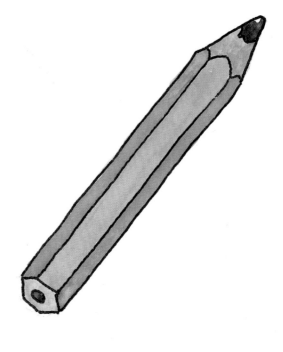

It is a pencil.

It is a fish.

It is a fly.

It is a flower.

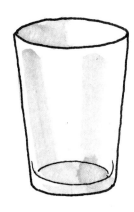

It is a glass.

It is an egg.

D d

desk   dog   doll

9

I am _____ .

I am _____ .

I am John.

I am Mary.

E e

desk   egg   pencil

I am Paul.
I am a boy.

I am Mimi.
I am a girl.

I am John.
I am a boy.

I am _____ .

I am Mary.
I am a girl.

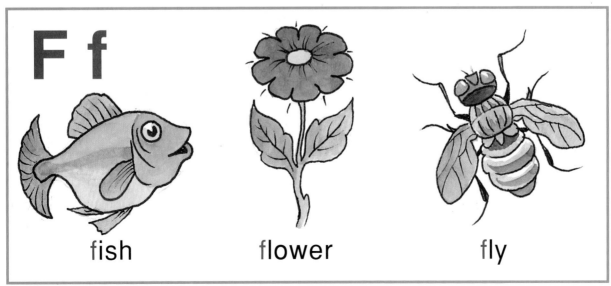

F f

fish   flower   fly

I am Paul.

You are Mimi.

I am Mimi.

You are Paul.

G g

glass

girl

This is Paul.
This is Mimi.

This is John.
This is Mary.

This is a man.

This is a woman.

This is a house.

This is a picture.

This is a hen.

This is a pin.

H h

hen

house

This is Paul.
He is a boy.

This is Mimi.
She is a girl.

This is John.
He is a boy.

This is Mary.
She is a girl.

This is Miss Lee.
She is a woman.
She is a teacher.

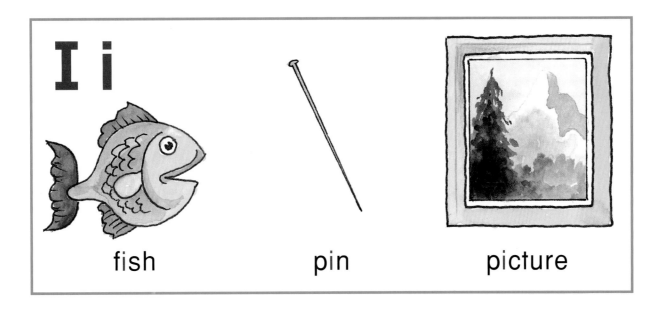

I i

fish   pin   picture

and

This is a pen and this is a pencil.

This is a banana and this is a cookie.

This is a kite and this is a car.

This is a lamp and this is a jar.

This is a bell and this is a flower.

This is a boat and this is a baby.

J j

jar

John

My name is Co-co.

my hair

my ear

my nose

my tooth

my neck

my eye

my lip

my mouth

my face

This is my head.

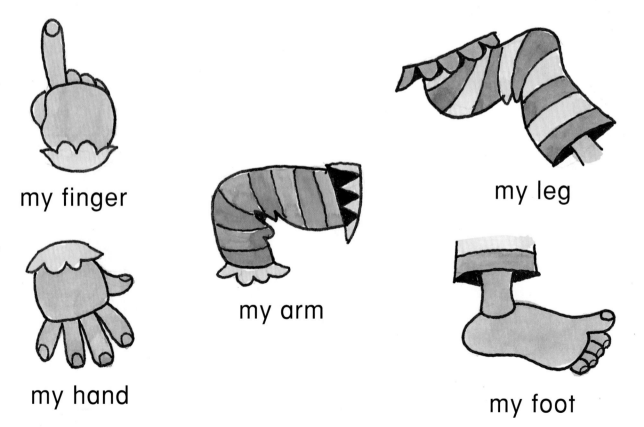

my finger

my arm

my leg

my hand

my foot

My name is Co-co.

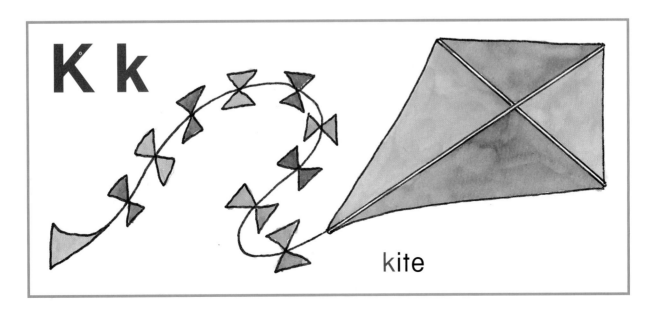

K k

kite

This is my chair.

This is your chair.

This is my desk.

This is your desk.

This is my umbrella.

This is your umbrella.

lamp

leg

This is Peter.

This is his kite.

This is Paul.

This is his father.   This is his mother.

This is Mimi.

This is her father.   This is her mother.

M m

mouth   man   Mimi and her mother

What is your name?

My name is Paul.

What is my name?

Your name is Mimi.

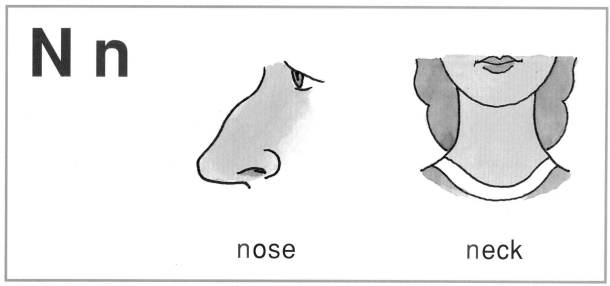

N n

nose   neck

What is it?

What is it?

It is a cake.

What is it?

It is a car.

What is it?

It is a clock.

What is it?

It is a pocket.

What is it?

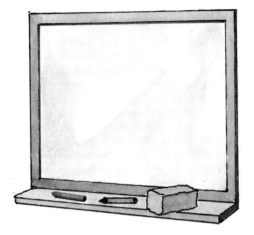

It is a whiteboard.

What is it?

It is a tree.

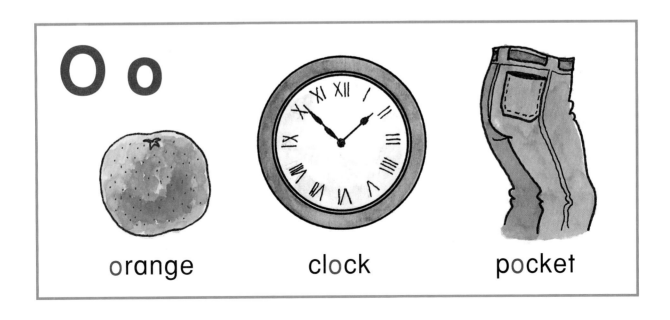

O o

orange   clock   pocket

What is this?
It is a pencil.

What is this?
It is a pen.

What is this?
It is an eraser.

What is this?   It is a ship.

P p

ship   pencil   pen

Is it a desk?
Is it a chair?

Is it a dog?
Is it a cat?

Is it a flower?
Is it a glass?

Is it a pen?
Is it a pencil?

Is it a cake?
Is it a clock?

Is it a hen?
Is it a fish?

Is it a bird?
Is it a ship?

Is it an egg?
Is it a bird?

Is it a leg?
Is it a foot?

Is it an arm?
Is it a hand?

Q q

queen

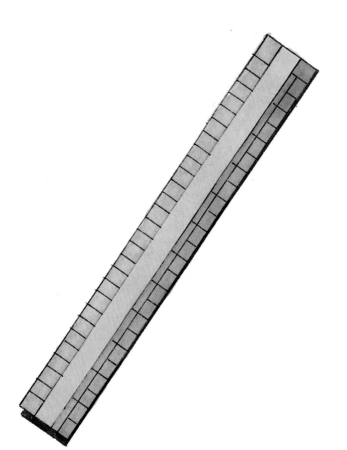

Is this a pencil?
No, it is not.

Is this an eraser?
No, it is not.

Is this a ruler?
Yes, it is.

Is this a cup?
No, it is not.

Is this a glass?
No, it is not.

Is this a knife?
Yes, it is.

Is this a ship?
No, it is not.

Is this a house?
No, it is not.

Is this a school?
Yes, it is.

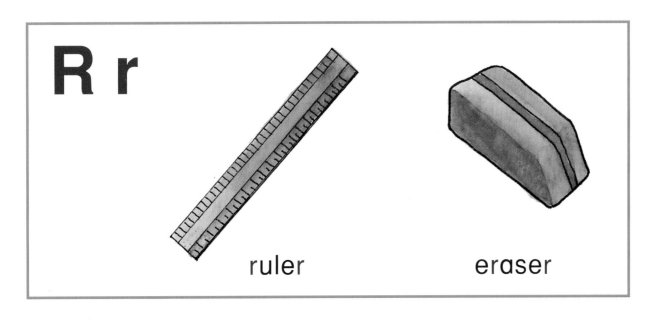

R r

ruler   eraser

37

Is he a mail carrier?
No, he is not.

Is he a teacher?
No, he is not.

Is he a police officer?
Yes, he is.

Is he a police officer?
No, he is not.

Is he a teacher?
No, he is not.

Is he a mail carrier?
Yes, he is.

38

Is she a girl?
No, she is not.

Is she a police officer?
No, she is not.

Is she a teacher?
Yes, she is.

S s

eraser

school

Is this a table?
No, it is not a table.
It is a chair.

Is this a table?
No, it is not a table.
It is a television.

Is this a chair?
No, it is not a chair.
It is a table.

He is not a _____ .

Is he a teacher?
No, he is not a teacher.
He is a mail carrier.

T t

table   television   teacher

It is _____ .

This is a bus.
It is yellow.

This is an umbrella.
It is green.

This is a flower.
It is white.

This is an apple.
It is red.

This is a bird.
It is blue.

This is a car.
It is black.

This is a cup.
It is white.

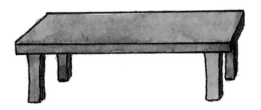

This is a table.
It is brown.

This is a chair.
It is brown.

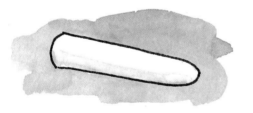

This is chalk.
It is white.

This is chalk.
It is red.

This is milk.
It is white.

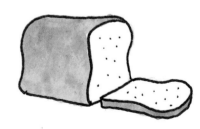

This is bread.
It is white.

43

This bag is big.

This bag is little.

This ruler is long.

This ruler is short.

This is milk.
It is hot.

This is ice cream.
It is cold.

This is water.
It is dirty.

This is water.
It is clean.

very _____

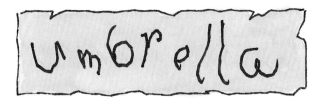 umbrella   This is bad.

umbrella   This is very bad.

umbrella   This is good.

umbrella   This is very good.

U u

cup   umbrella

He is tall.
He is very tall.

She is short.
She is very short.

His shirt is dirty.
It is very dirty.

Her dress is clean.
It is very clean.

He is old.
He is very old.

She is thin.
She is very thin.

She is very _____ .

Is she tall?
Yes, she is.
She is very tall.

Is he short?
Yes, he is.
He is very short.

Is he fat?
Yes, he is.
He is very fat.

very old

Please open the window.

Shut the window, please.

Please open the door.

Shut the door, please.

Please stand up.

Please sit down.

Hold up a book, please.

Please point to a wall.

Look at the board.

Knock on your desk.

Knock on the door.

Come Go Draw

 Come to my desk, please.

 Go to your desk, please.

 Please come to the door.

 Please go to the window.

 Please come to the board.

 Please draw a picture.

He is drawing.

She is writing.

He is walking.

She is running.

He is reading.

He is shouting.

He is playing.

She is playing.

I am _____ing.

I am _____ing.

Is he jumping?
Yes, he is.

Is he jumping?
No, he is not.

Is she clapping?
Yes, she is.

Is she clapping?
No, she is not.

Is she opening the window?
No, she is not.

Is he shutting the door?
No, he is not.

Is he crying?
Yes, he is.

Is she singing?
Yes, she is.

Is he eating?
Yes, he is.

Is she drinking?
Yes, she is.

Is she drinking?
No, she is not drinking.
She is crying.

Is he eating?
No, he is not eating.
He is singing.

I have a pen. He has a pencil.

I have a ball. She has a doll.

I have a cat. He has a dog.

I have a picture book. He has a storybook.

I have a book in my left hand.
I have a ruler in my right hand.

She has an apple in her left hand.
She has a basket in her right hand.

W w

window   woman   walking

This is Mimi.

This is her brother.   This is her sister.

This is Mr. Bell.

This is his son.   This is his daughter.

This is Mimi and
her friend.
They are playing.

This is Paul and
his friend.
They are playing.

Look at all the toys.
One doll is big. Point to it.

Point to all the toys.

One doll is small.
One dog is black.
One dog is white.
One ball is red.
One ball is green.
One ball is yellow.
One kite is big.
One kite is little.
One kite is green.

This is a room.

This is a classroom.

X x Y y Z z

yellow box   zebra

Word List

A
a, an	1, 3
all	59
am	10
and	20
apple	3
are	14
arm	22

B
baby	21
bad	45
bag	2
ball	1
banana	20
basket	57
bell	21
big	44
bird	35
black	43
blue	42
board	49
boat	21
book	1
box	4
boy	12
bread	43
brother	58
brown	43
bus	42

C
cake	30
car	6
cat	2
chair	24
chalk	43
clap	53
classroom	61
clean	44
clock	30
cold	44
come	50
cookie	20
cry	55
cup	4

D
daughter	58
desk	5
dirty	44
dog	6
doll	8
door	48
draw	50
dress	46
drink	55

E
ear	22
eat	55
egg	9
eraser	32
eye	22

F
face	22
fat	47
father	26
finger	22
fish	8
flower	9
fly	8
foot	22
friend	59

G
girl	12
glass	9
go	50
good	45
green	42

H
hair	22
hand	22
has	56
have	56
he	18
head	22
hen	17
her	27
his	26
hold up	49
hot	44
house	17

I
I	10
ice cream	44
in	57
is	6
it	6

J
jar	20
jump	53

Word List

K
kite	20
knife	36
knock on	49

L
lamp	20
left	57
leg	22
lip	22
little	44
long	44
look at	49

M
mail carrier	38
man	17
milk	43
Miss	19
mother	26
mouth	22
Mr.	29
my	22

N
name	22
neck	22
no	34
nose	22
not	36

O
old	46
one	59
open	48
orange	3

P
pen	20
pencil	8
picture	17
pin	17
play	51
please	48
pocket	30
point to	49
police officer	38

Q
queen	35

R
read	51
red	42
right	57
room	60
ruler	36
run	51

S
school	37
she	18
ship	33
shirt	46
shoe	25
short	44
shout	51
shut	48
sing	55
sister	58
sit down	48
son	58
stand up	48
storybook	56

T
table	40
tall	46
teacher	19
television	40
the	48
thin	46
this	16
tooth	22
toy	59
tree	31

U
umbrella	7

V
very	45

W
walk	51
wall	49
water	44
What?	28
white	42
whiteboard	31
window	48
woman	17
write	51

Y
yellow	42
yes	34
you	14
your	24

Z
zebra	62